Elegantly Easy
CREME BRULEE
&
Other Custard Desserts

Elegantly Easy

CREME BRULEE

&

Other Custard Desserts

DEBBIE PUENTE

RENAISSANCE BOOKS

Los Angeles

*This book is dedicated to
the eleven most important people in my life,
my family:
David, Joey, Steven, Cole, Evelyn, Shelly,
Iris, Judi, Beth, Jo, and Ralphie.*

Photo Credits: Brian Leatart: 13, 25, 41, 48, 57, 61, 73, 76, 81
Rob Outwater: cover, 20, 31, 34, 45, 52, 66, 83, 89

Prop Stylist: Ann Hartley

Food Stylists: Debbie Puente and Kimberly Huson: 13, 25, 41, 48, 57, 61, 73, 76, 81
Debbie Puente and Jill Freedman Gorelick: cover, 20, 31, 34, 45, 52, 66, 83, 89
Enrico Glaudo: cover, 66

Design: Deborah Daly

ACKNOWLEDGMENTS

The enjoyment of doing this book was greatly enhanced by all the people who participated in its creation. I would like to express my deep appreciation to:

My manager, Heidi Rotbart, for making the Renaissance connection, believing in me, and, most of all, for friendship and assistance throughout this project. Ann Hartley for the photo-shoot prop styling (and the props themselves!) and the awe-inspiring job of copyediting. Michael Levine for selling the concept of crème brûlée to Renaissance Books, and Bill Hartley, publisher of Renaissance Books, for his faith in the idea.

The talented Brian Leatart for his impressive photography and his calming influence in our first photo shoot. Recipe writer Brenda Koplin for her helpful guidance and, of course, Campion Primm for putting me in touch with Brian and Brenda. Kimberly Huson for the food styling in our first photo shoot.

In our second photo shoot, Rob Outwater for his expert photography and his generosity. Steve Burdick for beautiful flowers and general assistance. Jason Vishnefske and Matt Lansford of Santa Barbara Chocolates for supplying the wonderful chocolate. Chef Enrico Glaudo for preparing and styling his creation, and a very special thank-you to Jill Freedman Gorelick for helping me prepare and style the recipes.

Sandee Hall and Nicole Adler at the Williams-Sonoma store in Beverly Hills for the tasteful supplemental props; Victoria Kalish at Williams-Sonoma corporate for taking a chance on me; and my fellow co-workers and managers at Williams-Sonoma, especially Steven Sigur, for allowing flexibility in my schedule so I could work on this book.

Those who sampled recipes, and offered encouragement and support: Helene McCabe, Mary Kay McCartney, Debbie Berglas, Marla Grosslight, Patty Sweet, Teri Hinson, Linda Abbott, Ritz Sales, Wendy Herman, Debbie Copsey, and Rosie Vasquez. For proofreading and editing help: Judi Howard James, Iris Howard, and Barbara Howard. For encouragement and friendship from afar: Steve LeVine and Vanessa Webber.

Karen Spiegler and Bonnie Rice for affording me the opportunity to begin a career in culinary writing. And finally, a very special thank-you to those who paved the way, and educated and entertained me with expertise and wit for so long: The Housewife Writers of Prodigy's Books and Writing Board.

CONTENTS

Classic Crème Brûlée Spirit, Cordial, and Liqueur Variations (*cont.*)

SPECIAL PRESENTATIONS!

Introduction

The origins of crème brûlée (pronounced *krehm broo-LAY*) are very much in contention, with the English, Spanish, and French all staking claim. The Spanish have taken credit for this dessert as "crema catalana" since the eighteenth century, while the English claim it originated in seventeenth-century Britain, where it was known as "burnt cream." It apparently wasn't until the end of the nineteenth century that common usage of the French translation came into vogue, but its wide recognition today seems to have given the French credit for inventing crème brûlée. For this I thank them, because I just don't think there's a market for an *Elegantly Easy Burnt Cream* book.

Regardless of its origins, this delicate, silken, and sinfully rich dessert, which blends the cool velvet of custard with a crisp, caramelized topping, is now served in fine restaurants everywhere. But it is also simple and economical to make at home. For a traditional crème brûlée, you need nothing more than cream, eggs, sugar, and vanilla. And, as you'll discover in the following pages, a few additional ingredients can transform this elegant dessert into an extraordinary culinary creation.

In these recipes I will show you how to add a medley of aromatic spices, fruits, and citrus flavors, to create exciting and exotic variations on the basic theme. I'll also take you beyond crème brûlée to explore the wider world of caramel custards, flans, bread (croissant) pudding, and rice puddings. As well, four renowned chefs have each generously contributed their own unique recipe to this book.

Once you discover how truly easy these recipes are to prepare, elaborate upon, and personalize, you may even be tempted to stake a claim of your own.

Debbie Puente

The Basics

Cooking Methods

There are two basic ways to make crème brûlée.

In the first, the cream is blended with the other ingredients and then baked in gentle heat until set. Baking the custard produces a firm texture.

The second method involves cooking and stirring the cream on the stove, and is used when infusing flavors, or when you plan to serve your creation in an edible bowl or shell. This stovetop method produces a custard with a creamy texture.

In both methods, the custard should be chilled for at least two hours, then topped with sugar and quickly caramelized.

Ingredients

Cream

The grocery store offers an array of creams with varying amounts of butterfat: half-and-half (10.5 percent); light cream (18 percent); whipping cream (30 percent); heavy cream, also known as heavy whipping cream (36 percent); and double cream (48 percent). You may also want to try manufacturer's cream (40 percent butterfat), which is more economical and often available at warehouse grocery stores. A classic crème brûlée uses heavy whipping cream, but as you add rich ingredients, such as chocolate, you may prefer to use a lighter cream for balance. In any of these recipes, light cream, a mixture of cream and milk, or half-and-half can be substituted without affecting the taste.

Sugar

When sugar melts, it turns to caramel which, when cool, becomes very brittle. The caramelized top is the distinguishing feature of crème brûlée. Sugar comes in many forms: granulated (regular or table sugar), superfine (finely granulated), confectioners' (also known as powdered or icing sugar), light brown or dark brown (granulated sugar combined with molasses), and raw (unrefined). I tend to use whatever is on hand; either light brown sugar, which has been pre-dried, or superfine sugar have given me excellent results. Instructions for pre-drying brown sugar are discussed in **Tips and Techniques** (page 23).

Eggs

Always use grade A large eggs. Pay close attention to the date on the carton, and store in the refrigerator. Chilled eggs are easier to separate because the yolks are firmer. In general, my recipes call for 8 yolks per 2 cups of cream. This is for a very rich, traditional crème brûlée. You may choose to reduce the number of egg yolks listed in any recipe; you may prefer to use half as many yolks or even whole eggs instead. Unlike other baked desserts, custards are not all that fussy and are very forgiving.

Vanilla Beans / Vanilla Extract

Vanilla beans contain tiny seeds that add beauty and flavor. Vanilla extract is a more convenient form of vanilla; always use pure extract, not imitation. Madagascar Bourbon Pure Vanilla Extract, an exceptionally aromatic flavoring, is available at most food specialty shops.

Fruit

Whether tart, tangy, sweet, or juicy, fruit is the perfect accompaniment to the rich sweetness of crème brûlée. Use fruits in season for value and freshness.

Chocolate

Most domestic chocolates are not as high quality as the imported brands. Look for *couverture* quality, meaning it contains between 31 and 38 percent cocoa butter, and between 38 and 61 percent pure chocolate. Among the best are Callebaut and Valrhona.

Equipment

Whisk

Used with a swift, circular motion, this looped-wire kitchen utensil is the ideal tool for blending sauces, eggs, and other liquid ingredients. Whisks should be stainless steel so they don't rust, and should have wooden (or stay-cool) handles. Ideally, a whisk should be ten to twelve inches long and two inches across at the balloon end.

Strainer

For ultrasmooth, velvety custards, it is important to use a strainer. If you want the best, invest in a chinois (a metal conical strainer with an extremely fine mesh) and a dowel (a wooden tool used to force purées through the chinois). Even minute particles can't pass through.

Ramekins or Custard Cups

Although any ovenproof cup, including coffee cups or mugs, can be used to bake custards, traditional crème dishes are 4 inches in diameter and 3/4 inch deep. French porcelain ramekins (miniature soufflé dishes) seem to be the preference at restaurants and with most cooks. They're wonderful for individual soufflés and mousses as well as for crème brûlée. The porcelain ramekins are dishwasher- and microwave-safe, ovenproof, and they make a lovely presentation.

Large Pan or Casserole Dish

For foolproof, never-curdled, never-cracked custard, always use a water bath *(bain-marie)*. This is simply a large, shallow pan such as a roasting pan or even a large casserole dish of warm water, which surrounds the baking food with gentle, moist heat. This process is further explained in **Tips and Techniques** (page 21).

Double Boiler

A double boiler consists of two pans fitted one inside the other. The bottom pan holds simmering water, which gently heats the mixture in the upper pan. The temperature of the food never reaches the boiling point, hence heat-sensitive foods such as chocolate, delicate sauces, custards, or egg dishes will not overheat or curdle.

Another option, if you don't have a double boiler, is to improvise by setting a heatproof bowl over a saucepan of simmering water. At least one inch of air-space should be left between the water and the bowl. This space can be created by using a bowl slightly larger than the pan, so that the bottom of the bowl is suspended above, and never actually touches the water.

Oven Thermometer

This tool is essential for accuracy. Erroneous oven temperatures can create all kinds of culinary havoc. Overcooked custard has an extremely unpleasant texture, and an oven thermometer is a very inexpensive way to ensure a successful result.

Butane Torch

For caramelizing the tops of custards, the butane torch is the tool of choice for most professionals. It offers the best control and produces a glassy crust. The small, hand-held kitchen torch, available through the Williams-Sonoma catalog, has an adjustable flame that melts sugar quickly, so the custard beneath stays cool. This user-friendly tool is far less intimidating than the large blowtorches used in most restaurant kitchens.

Broiler

Your oven broiler will work fine for melting and caramelizing the sugar. The custards should be no more than five inches away from the heat source. If necessary, an inverted roasting pan can be used to elevate the custards and position them closer to the heat. Place custards on a baking sheet, or jellyroll pan, for easier handling. The sugar will melt in as little as two minutes, so watch carefully.

Salamander

Also used for caramelizing crème brûlée, the salamander is a tool that is heated and used somewhat like a branding iron to melt the sugar. Salamanders are available at most kitchen-supply stores.

TIPS AND TECHNIQUES

A water bath is the oven-equivalent of the double boiler. A paper towel placed on the bottom of the water-bath pan will prevent the ramekins from sliding. Place the custard-filled ramekins in the pan, and place on center rack of oven. Carefully fill the pan with warm water, until the level reaches halfway up the sides of the ramekins. Covering the pan tightly with aluminum foil will keep a skin from forming over the top of the custard.

Low, slow cooking will result in a smooth, silken texture, as well as prevent the possibility of curdling. Recommended cooking time is 40 to 50 minutes at 300°F, although, if you are in a hurry, 325°F for 25 to 30 minutes is an acceptable alternative.

A stirred custard is done when it leaves a velvety coating on the back of a wooden spoon or, if you dip your finger into it, the custard doesn't drip off. You must be sure the water gently simmering in the double boiler never comes to a boil, so the custard will never be so hot as to burn your finger. **A baked custard is done** just before it sets. The center should not yet be firm, and you should see a slight quiver in the center when the pan is moved (think Jell-O).

To salvage a curdled custard, pour the mixture into a food processor or blender immediately and start processing on lowest speed, increasing to high. It will smooth out perfectly in only seconds.

Exercise caution when removing custard from oven. To prevent scalding from any splashing water, use a long-handled ladle or basting bulb to lower the water level.

Allow custard to cool before refrigeration. Chill for at least two hours, or for as long as two days in advance.

To caramelize the tops of custards, heat the sugar until it liquefies and becomes syrupy. As it cools, the caramelized sugar hardens and quickly becomes brittle and can, therefore, crack very easily. Either white or brown sugar can be used, and it can be heated using any of the methods mentioned in **Equipment** (pages 19–20).

To perfect your caramelizing skills, begin with a small amount of sugar, melt it, then add another layer of sugar, melt, and repeat until you have reached the desired thickness.

When using the **hand-held torch,** hold it four to five inches away from the sugar, maintaining a slow and even motion. The sugar will quickly melt and caramelize; watch carefully so the custards do not burn.

Be extremely cautious when using the torch to caramelize any custard which contains alcohol. The burning alcohol could cause the caramelizing sugar to spatter. You may prefer to use the broiler method or the variation method below whenever alcohol is used as an ingredient in a recipe.

If using the **broiler method to caramelize,** it is best to place chilled custards in a pan filled with ice before caramelizing the tops. This will ensure cold, firm custards.

An interesting variation is to make the caramelized top in advance. Cut a piece of aluminum foil the exact size of the dish in which you plan to serve the brûlée. Butter the foil on one side. Firmly pat about ¼-inch-thickness of brown or white sugar, in a lacy, round pattern, onto the buttered foil. Place the foil on a baking sheet, sugared-side up. At this point the procedure needs your entire attention! Place baking sheet under the broiler heat until sugar is caramelized or glazed. This method can also be accomplished using the hand-held torch and, in fact, is easier.

Remove from oven and invert foil, with the sugar rounds, onto a cake rack to cool. When rounds are slightly cooled, the foil should peel off, leaving a large praline. Place the praline on the custard just before serving; the crust will disintegrate if put on the custard too early.

A note about using **brown sugar**: Due to the molasses content, it is recommended that brown sugar be pre-dried prior to the caramelizing process. This significantly improves the taste, texture, and appearance.

To get the brown sugar as dry as possible, spread thinly on a baking sheet and bake for about five minutes at 300°F. After the sugar has been removed from the oven and cooled, transfer to a small, plastic zip-close freezer bag. Seal the bag and finely crush the sugar with a rolling pin. Store sugar in an airtight container until it is needed.

When melting chocolate, it is important to remember that chocolate melts at a very low temperature (think of a candy bar left in a warm car). Because it retains its shape if left undisturbed, it is easy to assume that a longer cooking time may be required. Great care should be taken not to overheat; if overheated, the chocolate may scorch or turn grainy. When melting dark chocolate in a double boiler, keep water at a temperature below simmering and, after the chocolate liquefies, stir frequently until smooth. Milk or white chocolate should be stirred constantly. Remove top part of double boiler, or its equivalent (page 19), from heat.

In this book, I've also included recipes for rice pudding, flan, and crème caramel because they have a soft, creamy consistency and are based on a custard mixture. And since you'll have leftover egg whites after using only the yolks, the tulip-shell recipe is included as a wonderful way to use them. You can also save egg whites for preparing meringues or soufflés. They can be kept refrigerated for about a week, or frozen for up to six months.

Please! Use your imagination, with this book as a basic guide. If the Lavender Flower Crème Brûlée sounds appealing to you, then why not also try other edible flowers, such as anise, chamomile, geraniums, honeysuckle, pansies, or violets? If citrus is your thing, you could also try key lime, lemon, kiwi, or even grapefruit as options to the orange in the Orange Cardamom recipe.

The Recipes

≈ Classic Crème Brûlée ≈

A straightforward and unpretentious creation that is so simple, so rich, so praised!

8 egg yolks
⅓ cup granulated white sugar
2 cups heavy cream

1 teaspoon pure vanilla extract
¼ cup granulated white sugar
   (for the caramelized tops)

Preheat oven to 300°F. In a large bowl, whisk together egg yolks and sugar until the sugar has dissolved and the mixture is thick and pale yellow. Add cream and vanilla, and continue to whisk until well blended. Strain into a large bowl, skimming off any foam or bubbles.

Divide mixture among 6 ramekins or custard cups. Place in a water bath (page 21), and bake until set around the edges, but still loose in the center, about 40 to 50 minutes. Remove from oven and leave in the water bath until cooled. Remove cups from water bath and chill for at least 2 hours, or up to 2 days.

When ready to serve, sprinkle about 2 teaspoons of sugar over each custard. For best results, use a small, hand-held torch to melt sugar. If you don't have a torch, place under the broiler until sugar melts. Re-chill custards for a few minutes before serving. *Serves 6.*

❧ Classic Crème Brûlée, ❧ Stirred Method

Cooking and stirring will produce a custard with a creamy texture. This method is best if you want to use the edible fancy presentation cups (page 90), or when you are making custard to be used in a pie-filling.

8 egg yolks
⅓ cup granulated white sugar
2 cups heavy cream
1 teaspoon pure vanilla extract,

or 1 whole vanilla bean, split in
half lengthwise
¼ cup granulated white sugar
(for the caramelized tops)

In a large bowl, whisk together egg yolks and sugar until the sugar has dissolved and the mixture is thick and pale yellow. Set aside. Using a double boiler, or a heatproof bowl set over gently simmering water (page 19), bring the cream to a gentle simmer; do not boil. Remove the cream from heat, and slowly pour into egg mixture. Add vanilla.

Pour mixture into top of double boiler; the water should be simmering, not boiling. Cook, stirring frequently, until the custard is thick enough to coat the back of a wooden spoon, about 30 minutes. Remove from heat and strain into a large, clean bowl. The custard will thicken as it cools. Chill completely, at least 6 hours.

When ready to serve, fill individual serving containers, such as ramekins, custard cups, coffee cups, or edible serving cups, with the chilled custard. Sprinkle about 2 teaspoons of sugar over each custard, and caramelize. For best results, use the small, hand-held torch to melt sugar. *Serves 6.*

❧ Classic Crème Brûlée ❧ Fruit Variations

There are endless variations to mixing fruit with the Classic Crème Brûlée. It is best to start with the Classic Crème Brûlée, Stirred Method. Place fruit, or fruit mixtures, evenly on the bottom of the ramekins or custard cups. Top with cooled custard and proceed with the caramelizing. Before caramelizing custards which contain alcohol, please see note in **Tips and Techniques** (page 22).

Dutch Apple

Peel and core two Granny Smith apples, or any other variety of tart apple, and cut into bite-size pieces. Put apples into a small saucepan, along with 2 tablespoons of ground cinnamon, ¼ cup granulated white sugar, and ¼ cup water. Cook mixture over low heat for about 10 minutes, or until apples have softened. Chill until ready to use.

Bananas Foster

Slice two ripe bananas into bite-size pieces and place in a bowl. Mix ½ stick (4 tablespoons) melted unsalted butter with 3 tablespoons of brown sugar. Add 3 tablespoons dark rum and mix well. Pour mixture over bananas, coating completely. Arrange bananas flat-side down in ramekins. Spoon chilled custard over top and proceed with caramelizing.

Papayas or Mangoes

These luscious fruits, with their juicy, velvety flesh, are wonderful on their own or mixed with other fruits, such as bananas. With these cut up and placed at the bottom of the crème brûlée, your creation will be exotic as well as delicious. Papayas and mangoes would also complement the Caribbean Crème Brûlée (page 65).

Amaretto or Brandy Peach

Pour 2 tablespoons amaretto liqueur or ¼ cup brandy over 4 medium-size peaches, sliced. Place in a single layer on the bottom of serving container, spooning custard over the peaches.

Rum Raisin

Mix ½ cup raisins with ½ cup dark rum, following the instructions above.

Berries

Blackberries, boysenberries, blueberries, raspberries, and strawberries are all perfect with crème brûlée.

❧ CLASSIC CRÈME BRÛLÉE ❧
SPIRIT, CORDIAL, AND LIQUEUR VARIATIONS

Crème brûlée and after-dinner drinks have long been enjoyed as the finishing touch and delightful end to a leisurely repast. Both are lingered over, savored, and consumed slowly, so it makes sense to combine them!

Start with the recipe for Classic Crème Brûlée, blending the following mixtures in with the cream and vanilla. The amounts given are for a mild, light flavor. Adjust amounts to your liking. Because these variations all contain alcohol, before caramelizing please see note in **Tips and Techniques** (page 22).

AMARETTO

Mix 3 tablespoons amaretto, plus ⅛ teaspoon almond extract, into the cream.

BOURBON

Mix ¼ cup good-quality bourbon whiskey with the cream.

COGNAC

Mix ¼ cup cognac with the cream.

GRAND MARNIER

Mix 3 tablespoons Grand Marnier, plus the zest of one orange, into the cream. Allow oils from the zest to seep into the cream for at least 15 minutes. Strain before dividing the mixture into ramekins.

KAHLUA

Mix ¼ cup Kahlua, plus ¼ tablespoon instant espresso powder, into the cream.

CASSIS

Mix 2 tablespoons cassis, plus ½ cup black currant preserves, into the cream. Strain before dividing the mixture into ramekins.

WHITE RUSSIAN

Mix 2 tablespoons vodka and 2 tablespoons Kahlua into the cream.

IRISH COFFEE

Mix 1 tablespoon Irish whiskey, plus 1 heaping tablespoon (about 4 teaspoons) instant coffee, into the cream.

IRISH CREAM

Mix 3 tablespoons good-quality Irish Cream, such as Bailey's or Emmet's, with the cream.

FRANGELICO

Mix 2 tablespoons Frangelico with the cream. Option: Add 1 heaping tablespoon (about 4 teaspoons) instant coffee.

MARGARITA

Mix 3 tablespoons tequila, 2 tablespoons orange liqueur (such as Grand Marnier or Triple Sec), and 2 tablespoons lime juice into the cream.

MISSISSIPPI MUD

Mix 2 tablespoons Southern Comfort and 2 tablespoons coffee liqueur into the cream.

❧ Crème Brûlée Chaude ❧ avec des Fruits

This inventive, hot crème brûlée with fresh fruits has become one of the trademarks of La Brasserie restaurant in Washington, D.C. Serving classic and regional French cuisine since 1979, La Brasserie is a favorite with the Capitol Hill gang.

1 whole egg
4 egg yolks
½ cup granulated white sugar
1 tablespoon vanilla extract
2 cups heavy cream
6 large strawberries, sliced

3 kiwis, peeled and sliced
1 cup raspberries
2 oranges, peeled and sliced
⅓ cup brown sugar (for the
  caramelized tops)

Preheat oven to 275°F. In a large bowl, combine eggs and sugar, and whip for 5 minutes. Add vanilla and cream, mixing until texture is smooth. Pour into an ovenproof baking dish, and place in a water bath (page 21). Bake for about 1 hour and 15 minutes. Remove from oven and leave in water bath until cooled.

Transfer approximately 1 cup of the cooled custard to each of 6 ovenproof serving plates and top with sliced strawberries, sliced kiwis, raspberries, and sliced oranges, or any variation you may prefer. Sprinkle each with 1 tablespoon of brown sugar, and broil for 5 minutes or, if desired, use the hand-held torch. Serve hot. *Serves 6.*

❦ NONFAT CRÈME BRÛLÉE ❦

Make this recipe extra special by adding your favorite fruits or liqueurs. For suggestions, see the preceding Crème Brûlée Fruit Variations and the Crème Brûlée Spirit, Cordial, and Liqueur Variations.

2 cups nonfat milk
2 tablespoons nonfat dry milk
  powder
1 cup frozen whole-egg
  substitute, thawed

⅓ cup granulated white sugar
1 teaspoon pure vanilla extract
¼ cup granulated white sugar
  (for the caramelized tops)

Preheat oven to 350°F. Mix ½ cup nonfat milk with the dry milk. Whisk in remaining milk, egg substitute, sugar, and vanilla. Blend well. Strain into a large bowl, skimming off any foam or bubbles.

Divide mixture among 6 ramekins or custard cups. Place in a water bath (page 21), and bake until set around the edges, but still loose in the center, about 40 to 50 minutes. Remove from oven and leave in the water bath until cooled. Remove cups from water bath and chill for at least 2 hours, or up to 2 days.

When ready to serve, sprinkle about 2 teaspoons of sugar over each custard. For best results, use a small, hand-held torch to melt sugar. If you don't have a torch, place under the broiler until sugar melts. Re-chill custards for a few minutes before serving. *Serves 6.*

❧ MILK CHOCOLATE CARAMEL ❧ CRÈME BRÛLÉE

The irresistible combination of chocolate and caramel makes this one of my most-requested desserts. You may, if you prefer, substitute bittersweet or semisweet for the milk chocolate. (To clean the pan after making caramel, simply fill with water and bring to a boil.)

1 cup milk
1 cup heavy cream
1 cup granulated white sugar
1 tablespoon corn syrup
4 ounces good-quality milk
  chocolate

8 egg yolks
¼ cup granulated white sugar
  (for the caramelized tops)
milk chocolate shavings
  (optional)
fresh mint leaves (optional)

Combine the milk and cream in a medium saucepan and bring to a boil. Reduce heat to low, keeping the mixture hot.

Meanwhile, in a heavy saucepan, combine sugar and corn syrup. Add enough water to just cover the sugar mixture. Without stirring, cook over medium heat until the temperature reaches 356°F on a candy thermometer, or until mixture turns a deep amber color (this will take about 20 minutes). Remove from heat. While stirring the sugar mixture, *slowly and carefully* pour in the cream mixture; if poured too quickly, the mixture will spatter, and could cause severe burns. When all the cream is added, stir well to fully incorporate. Add the chocolate and stir until melted.

Preheat oven to 300°F. Place the egg yolks in a medium-size bowl. While stirring, slowly add the cream mixture to the yolks until completely blended. Divide mixture among 6 ramekins or custard cups. Place in a water bath (page 21), and bake until set around the edges, but still loose in the center, about 30 to 40 minutes. Remove from oven and leave in the water bath until cooled. Remove cups from water bath and chill for at least 2 hours, or up to 2 days.

When ready to serve, sprinkle about 2 teaspoons of sugar over each custard. For best results, use a small, hand-held torch to melt sugar. If you don't have a torch, place under the broiler until sugar melts. Rechill custards for a few minutes before serving. Garnish, if desired, with the chocolate shavings (made by shaving chocolate with a vegetable peeler) and fresh mint leaves. *Serves 6.*

❧ CARAMEL CRÈME BRÛLÉE ❧ VARIATIONS

When first experimenting with the preceding Milk Chocolate Caramel recipe I had many happy accidents. The following recipes are a few examples. All of these variations start with the Milk Chocolate Caramel Crème Brûlée, with slight changes in each, as noted. Before caramelizing custards which contain alcohol, please see note in **Tips and Techniques** (page 22).

BUTTERSCOTCH CARAMEL CRÈME BRÛLÉE

Omit the chocolate. Just after adding the cream, add ½ cup (1 stick) butter, 2 tablespoons Scotch whisky, and 1 teaspoon vanilla.

Light and Lowfat Milk Chocolate Caramel Crème Brûlée

The caramel custard has such an intense caramel flavor, so rich and satisfying, that you can lighten it and still get rave reviews. Simply substitute nonfat milk for the whole milk and cream, and use whole-egg substitute in place of egg yolks.

Milk Chocolate and Orange Caramel Crème Brûlée

Add the zest of one orange, plus 3 tablespoons of Grand Marnier, to cooled caramel-cream mixture. Strain out zest if desired.

Orange Caramel Crème Brûlée

Omit the chocolate and add the zest of one orange, plus 3 tablespoons of Grand Marnier, to cooled caramel-cream mixture. Strain out zest if desired.

Chocolate Caramel Fudge Sauce

Use 2 cups heavy cream instead of the 1 cup milk and 1 cup cream, and omit the eggs. The baking step is also not needed for this recipe.

❧ CHOCOLATE ESPRESSO ❧ CRÈME BRÛLÉE

For this recipe I suggest using espresso coffee-bean candies as a garnish, for an interesting (and literal) presentation.

2 cups heavy cream
1 tablespoon instant
  espresso powder
5 ounces bittersweet
  chocolate
6 egg yolks

3 tablespoons granulated white
  sugar
1 teaspoon pure vanilla extract
¼ cup granulated white sugar
  (for the caramelized tops)
espresso coffee-bean
  candies, for garnish

Preheat oven to 300°F. Combine cream and espresso powder in a heavy, medium saucepan. Bring to a simmer, whisking to dissolve espresso powder. Remove from heat. Break up chocolate and add to hot cream mixture, whisking until smooth. Set aside. Whisk yolks, sugar, and vanilla in a large bowl until well blended. Gradually whisk in chocolate mixture. Strain into a clean bowl, skimming off any foam or bubbles.

Divide mixture among 6 ramekins or custard cups. Place in a water bath (page 21), and bake until set around the edges, but still loose in the center, about 40 to 50 minutes. Remove from oven and leave in the water bath until cooled. Remove cups from water bath.

These custards can be served warm or chilled. To chill, refrigerate for at least 2 hours, or up to 2 days. When ready to serve, sprinkle about 2 teaspoons of sugar over each custard. For best results, use a small,

hand-held torch to melt sugar. If you don't have a torch, place under the broiler until sugar melts.

To serve warm, dry off bottoms of ramekins as soon as you remove them from the hot water bath, and present them plain. If desired, top warm crème brûlée with a generous dollop of freshly-whipped cream, or serve with vanilla ice cream.

Garnish with a sprinkling of coffee-bean candies. *Serves 6.*

✍ CHOCOLATE MINT CRÈME BRÛLÉE ✍

If you have an herb garden, pick your mint in the morning. Herbs picked early yield much more flavor.

2 cups whole fresh mint leaves,
   removed from stems and
   loosely packed
2 cups heavy cream
4 ounces good-quality bittersweet chocolate
8 egg yolks

⅓ cup granulated white sugar
3 tablespoons peppermint
   schnapps
¼ cup crushed peppermint
   candy or granulated sugar
   (for the caramelized tops)

Coarsely chop mint leaves; there should be about 1 cup after chopping. In a large saucepan, combine the cream and mint leaves, and bring to a gentle simmer. Remove from heat. Cover, and let flavors infuse for 30 minutes. Strain and discard mint leaves.

Preheat oven to 300°F. Coarsely chop chocolate. Melt in the top of a double boiler, or in a heatproof bowl over a pan of simmering water (page 19), stirring frequently. Turn off heat and let chocolate stand over warm water until ready to use. In a large bowl, beat together egg yolks and sugar for a few minutes, until sugar has dissolved and the mixture is thick and pale yellow. Set aside.

Slowly pour cream into egg mixture, whisking continuously. Strain through a fine-mesh strainer into a bowl. Stir in melted chocolate until mixture is smooth and well combined. Add peppermint schnapps. Divide mixture among 6 ramekins or custard cups. Place in a water bath (page 21), and bake until set around the edges, but still loose in the center, about 40 to 50 minutes. Remove from oven and leave in the water bath until cooled. Remove cups from water bath and chill for at least 2 hours, or up to 2 days.

When ready to serve, sprinkle 1 or 2 teaspoons of the crushed peppermint candy, or the sugar, evenly over the custards. Before caramelizing custards which contain alcohol, please see note in **Tips and Techniques** (page 22). After caramelizing, re-chill custards for a few minutes before serving. *Serves 6*

❧ CHOCOLATE AND BLACKBERRY TART ❧ CRÈME BRÛLÉE

Summer berries make a perfect match for a flaky tart shell lined with chocolate and filled with rich, creamy custard. Strawberries, raspberries, or blueberries could be substituted for the blackberries.

9-inch tart pan lined with Basic Pie Crust, baked (page 46)
6 egg yolks
6 tablespoons granulated white sugar
2 cups whipping cream

1 cup sour cream
1 teaspoon vanilla
3 ounces bittersweet chocolate
2 cups blackberries
¼ cup granulated white sugar (for the caramelized top)

In a large bowl, whisk together yolks, sugar, cream, sour cream, and vanilla. Transfer mixture to the top of a double boiler, or a heatproof bowl set over a pan of simmering water (page 19). Cook, stirring constantly, until the custard thickens, about 30 minutes. When custard is thick enough to coat the back of a wooden spoon, remove from heat and strain into a large, clean bowl. The custard will thicken as it cools. Keep custard chilled until ready to use.

Melt chocolate (page 23) and spread over the baked crust. Cover with berries. Top with cooled custard, smoothing with the back of a spoon or a spatula.

When ready to serve, sift sugar over entire top. For best results, use a small, hand-held torch to melt sugar. If you don't have a torch, place under the broiler until sugar melts. Re-chill tart for a few minutes before serving. *Serves 6 to 8.*

❧ BASIC PIE CRUST ❧

1 ¼ cups all-purpose flour
½ teaspoon salt
1 teaspoon granulated white
 sugar
6 tablespoons cold unsalted
 butter, cut into small pieces

2 tablespoons cold margarine
 or white vegetable shortening, cut into small pieces
2 to 4 tablespoons ice water

Place the flour, salt, and sugar in the bowl of a food processor fitted with the metal blade. Process 6 seconds, just to blend. Sprinkle the pieces of butter and margarine, or white vegetable shortening, over the surface and process 10 to 15 seconds, until the mixture resembles coarse crumbs.

Sprinkle 2 tablespoons of the ice water over flour mixture, and use pulse button to process until the dough just begins to hold together, 10 to 15 seconds. Test the dough by pinching a piece between your fingers. If it seems dry and crumbly, add more water, a little at a time, and pulse again until the dough becomes sticky. Turn dough onto a sheet of plastic wrap. Lightly press the dough into a disk shape, and flatten slightly. Wrap tightly and refrigerate at least 1 hour, or overnight.

Preheat oven to 400°F. Unwrap the dough and roll out on a lightly-floured surface to form an 11-inch circle. Transfer to a 9-inch pie plate or tart pan. Press the dough onto the bottom and up the sides. Trim dough, leaving a 1-inch overhang. Fold overhang toward the inside, and crimp edges. Pierce the bottom with a fork.

Cut a circle out of foil or waxed paper, about 3 inches larger than the pie plate or tart pan. Press onto the bottom and into edges of dough. Fill the paper- or foil-lined tart shell with dried beans, rice, or pastry weights, being careful to spread them evenly over bottom; weights will prevent the pastry from becoming puffy. Bake for 8 to 10 minutes.

Remove foil or waxed paper, and the weights, and return to oven. Bake until golden brown, about 12 minutes. Cool before filling. *Yields one 9-inch crust*

❧ White Chocolate Crème Brûlée ❧ with Peppermint

For most of the recipes in this book, many of the serving ideas in Special Presentations (page 90) could be substituted for the traditional ramekins. For this photo, I used a Chocolate Box, which could also be made with white chocolate instead of the dark.

8 ounces good-quality white chocolate, such as Callebaut
3 tablespoons granulated white sugar
3 tablespoons peppermint schnapps
6 egg yolks

2 cups heavy cream
3 to 4 tablespoons crushed peppermint candies, such as candy canes (for the caramelized tops)
fresh berries for garnish

Place the white chocolate in a double boiler, or in a heatproof bowl set over a pan of simmering water (page 19), and stir constantly until melted. Remove from heat. Whisk in sugar, peppermint schnapps, yolks, and cream, blending very well. Strain into a large bowl, skimming off any foam or bubbles.

Divide mixture among 6 ramekins or custard cups. Place in a water bath (page 21), and bake until set around the edges, but still loose in the center, about 40 to 50 minutes. Remove from oven and leave in the water bath until cooled. Remove cups from water bath and chill for at least 2 hours, or up to 2 days.

When ready to serve, sprinkle 1 or 2 teaspoons of the crushed peppermint candy evenly over each custard. Before caramelizing custards which contain alcohol, please see note in **Tips and Techniques** (page 22). Heat until candy melts. After caramelizing, re-chill custards for a few minutes before serving. Garnish with fresh berries.

For a romantic and extra-special presentation, spoon custard into chocolate boxes (page 91, and as shown in photo), caramelizing the tops using only the variation method described on page 22. *Serves 6*

White Chocolate–Macadamia Nut Crème Brûlée

Buttery, rich macadamia nuts, contrasted with the cool, smooth custard, creates a truly sensuous mélange of textures.

- 8 ounces good-quality white chocolate, such as Callebaut
- 3 tablespoons granulated white sugar
- 6 egg yolks
- 2 cups heavy cream
- 1 tablespoon pure vanilla extract
- 2 tablespoons macadamia nut liqueur (optional)
- ½ cup chopped macadamia nuts, toasted
- ¼ cup granulated white sugar (for the caramelized tops)

Preheat oven to 300°F. Place the white chocolate in a double boiler, or in a heatproof bowl set over a pan of simmering water (page 19), stirring constantly until melted. Remove from heat. Whisk in sugar, egg yolks, cream, vanilla, and (optional) macadamia nut liqueur. Blend very well.

To toast macadamia nuts, spread them out in a thin layer on a baking sheet. Place in a 300°F oven for 10 to 12 minutes, until lightly browned. Shake baking sheet a few times to toast the nuts evenly. Watch closely to make sure the nuts do not burn.

Divide the chopped toasted macadamia nuts among 6 ramekins or custard cups, and pour mixture over nuts. Place ramekins or custard cups in a water bath (page 21), and bake until set around the edges, but still loose in the center, about 40 to 50 minutes. Remove from oven and leave in the water bath until cooled. Remove cups from water bath and chill for at least 2 hours, or up to 2 days.

When ready to serve, sprinkle 1 or 2 teaspoons of sugar evenly over each custard. Before caramelizing custards which contain alcohol, please see note in **Tips and Techniques** (page 22). After caramelizing, re-chill custards for a few minutes before serving. *Serves 6*

≈ LAVENDER FLOWER CRÈME BRÛLÉE ≈

This very popular dessert on the menu at Café Provençal in Thousand Oaks, California, was created by Florence and Serge Bonnet, who opened this favorite Conejo Valley restaurant in 1994. The Bonnets, natives of France, tell me that lavender is the flower of Provence; it has a delicate and subtle fragrance, "the perfect ingredient for a crème brûlée." In the photo it is shown served in a Botanical Ice Bowl (page 95).

4 cups heavy cream	½ cup granulated white sugar
½ ounce dried lavender flower	¼ cup granulated white sugar
8 egg yolks	(for the caramelized tops)

Preheat oven to 300°F. In a large, heavy-bottomed saucepan, bring the cream and the lavender to a gentle boil. Remove from heat and allow the lavender to infuse with the cream for about 3 or 4 minutes. Meanwhile, whisk the egg yolks with the sugar until light and creamy. Remove the lavender and discard. Slowly pour the cream into the egg and sugar mixture, blending well. Strain into a large bowl, skimming off any foam or bubbles.

Divide mixture among 6 ramekins or custard cups. Place them in a water bath (page 21), and bake until set around the edges, but still loose in the center, about 40 to 50 minutes. Remove from oven and leave in the water bath until cooled. Remove cups from water bath and chill for at least 2 hours, or up to 2 days.

When ready to serve, sprinkle about 2 teaspoons of sugar over each custard. For best results, use a small, hand-held torch to melt sugar. If you don't have a torch, place under the broiler until sugar melts. Rechill custards for a few minutes before serving.

To serve in Botanical Ice Bowls, bake the custard in one large, oven-proof baking dish and place in water bath. When custard is well-chilled, spoon into the ice bowls and caramelize using the variation method described on page 22. *Serves 6*

❧ ROSE-SCENTED CRÈME BRÛLÉE ❧

Substitute 6 large, clean rose petals, or 1 tablespoon rose water, for the lavender flower. There is no need to cook the cream if you use the rose water.

⋙ ORANGE CARDAMOM CRÈME BRÛLÉE ⋘

Cardamom, a Far Eastern spice, adds a fragrant, cinnamon-like taste to this slightly tart creation.

6 egg yolks
4 tablespoons granulated white sugar
2 cups whipping cream
1 tablespoon vanilla
2 tablespoons orange liqueur, such as Triple Sec or Grand Marnier

2 tablespoons finely-grated orange zest (about 2 oranges)
4 to 5 crushed cardamom seeds (about 1 teaspoon)
¼ cup granulated white sugar (for the caramelized tops)

Preheat oven to 300°F. In a large bowl, whisk together egg yolks and sugar until the sugar has dissolved and the mixture is thick and pale yellow. Whisk in whipping cream, vanilla, orange liqueur, orange zest, and cardamom. Combine well.

Divide mixture among 6 ramekins or custard cups. Place in a water bath (page 21), and bake until set around the edges, but still loose in the center, about 40 to 50 minutes. Remove from oven and leave in the water bath until cooled. Remove cups from water bath and chill for at least 2 hours, or up to 2 days.

When ready to serve, sprinkle about 2 teaspoons of sugar over each custard. Before caramelizing custards which contain alcohol, please see note in **Tips and Techniques** (page 22). After caramelizing, re-chill custards for a few minutes before serving. *Serves 6.*

NOTE: A good-quality citrus zester is the easiest way to get thin strands of citrus zest. Press firmly as you draw the zester down along the skin of the fruit.

❦ FRENCH LEMON CUSTARD ❦ CRÈME BRÛLÉE

For the photo, I used strips of fresh lemon peel for garnish, but the presentation of this recipe can be made even more interesting with the Candied Lemon Zest garnish, described in the recipe that follows.

6 egg yolks
2 eggs
1 cup granulated white sugar
¼ cup fresh lemon juice
finely-grated zest of 2 lemons

2 cups heavy cream
¼ cup granulated white sugar
    (for the caramelized tops)
lemon peel for garnish, or
    Candied Lemon Zest

Preheat oven to 300°F. In a large bowl, combine yolks, eggs, and sugar. Whisk until smooth. Stir in lemon juice, zest, and cream. Allow oils from the zest to seep into the custard mixture for about 10 to 15 minutes. Strain into a large bowl, skimming off any foam or bubbles.

Divide mixture among 6 ramekins or custard cups. Place in a water bath (page 21), and bake until set around the edges, but still loose in the center, about 40 to 50 minutes. Remove from oven and leave in the water bath until cooled. Remove cups from water bath and chill for at least 2 hours, or up to 2 days.

When ready to serve, sprinkle about 2 teaspoons of sugar over each custard. For best results, use a small, hand-held torch to melt sugar. If you don't have a torch, place under the broiler until sugar melts. Re-chill custards for a few minutes before serving. Garnish with thin strips of fresh lemon peel, or Candied Lemon Zest. *Serves 6.*

❧ CANDIED LEMON ZEST ❧

3 or 4 lemons
1½ cups water, divided

1 cup sugar
2 tablespoons light corn syrup

With a sharp paring knife, cut the peel of 3 or 4 lemons in the size or shape you desire. (I generally cut into thin strips.) Combine with 1 cup of the water, and bring to a boil. Reduce heat and simmer until the peel is soft, about 15 minutes. Drain the water and, when the peel has cooled, carefully scrape off any white pith with a spoon; only the yellow-colored zest should remain. Combine the lemon peel, sugar, remaining water, and light corn syrup in the saucepan. Cook over medium heat until mixture is clear and registers 230°F on a candy thermometer. Drain and set aside until ready to use. *Yields enough for 6 servings.*

❧ Eggnog Crème Brûlée ❧

This recipe might make an interesting and unusual way to serve eggnog to your guests during the Christmas season!

2 cups heavy cream
1 cup whole milk
1 teaspoon fresh ground nutmeg
1 vanilla bean, split and scraped
8 egg yolks

⅔ cup granulated white sugar
¼ cup bourbon
¼ cup rum
¼ cup granulated white sugar
   (for the caramelized tops)

In a large saucepan, scald (heating to just below boiling point, until a skin forms over top) the cream, milk, nutmeg, and vanilla bean. Use all of the vanilla bean, including seeds. Remove from heat, cover, and let flavors *marry* (infuse) for at least 30 minutes. In a large bowl, whisk together egg yolks and sugar until the sugar has dissolved and the mixture is thick and pale yellow. Set aside. Reheat cream mixture to scalding, and slowly pour hot cream into egg mixture, whisking continuously. Pour entire mixture back into saucepan.

Reduce heat to very low, and return mixture to heat, stirring constantly with a wooden spoon until mixture thickens enough to coat the back of the spoon, about 40 minutes. Strain through a fine-mesh strainer into a bowl. Stir in bourbon and rum. Chill for at least 2 hours, or up to 2 days.

When ready to serve, divide custards evenly among 8 ramekins or custard cups. Sprinkle about 2 teaspoons of sugar over each custard. Before caramelizing custards which contain alcohol, please see note in **Tips and Techniques** (page 22). After caramelizing, re-chill custards for a few minutes before serving. *Serves 8.*

≈ STACKED BANANA CRÈME BRÛLÉE ≈ TOSTADA WITH CAJETA

Stephen Pyles, chef-owner of Star Canyon restaurant in Dallas, developed this Southwest-style dessert. The delightful flavor combinations will dazzle your taste buds!

4 egg yolks
4 tablespoons granulated white
  sugar
1½ cups heavy cream
¼ vanilla bean, split in half
  lengthwise

2 tablespoons dark rum
Tostada Rounds (page 62)
Candied Pecans (page 62)
Caramelized Bananas (page 63)
Cajeta (page 63)

In a double boiler or a large, heatproof bowl set over gently simmering water (page 19), whisk egg yolks and 3 tablespoons of the sugar vigorously until the mixture thickens, forms a ribbon when whisk is lifted, and resembles a thick hollandaise sauce. Remove bowl from heat briefly if the mixture gets too hot and starts to cook too rapidly around the edges. It is essential the yolks be heated through.

In a saucepan, bring the cream and vanilla bean to a boil. Slowly strain into the egg-yolk mixture while stirring. Cook over barely simmering water for 40 to 45 minutes, stirring occasionally, until the custard is slightly thickened. The heat should be very low and the custard should never be too hot to the touch. The mixture is cooked when it heavily coats the back of a wooden spoon. Strain through a fine sieve into a bowl set over ice, or chill in the refrigerator for at least 2 hours, or overnight.

❧ TOSTADA ROUNDS ❧

Tostada rounds are crispy fried tortillas.

12 flour tortillas, cut into
   3-inch circles
vegetable oil, for frying

4 tablespoons granulated sugar
2 tablespoons cinnamon
powdered sugar for dusting

In a medium saucepan, heat the vegetable oil until lightly smoking. Meanwhile, in a small mixing bowl, combine the granulated sugar and the cinnamon. Fry the flour tortillas in the oil, turning often until crisp and golden, about 3 minutes. Remove from the oil, place on a paper towel to drain excess oil, and sprinkle with the cinnamon-sugar mixture.

Dust 4 tortilla rounds with powdered sugar and, using a small butane torch or placing under the broiler, caramelize the dusted sugar. Set aside until needed.

❧ CANDIED PECANS ❧

1 cup pecans
1 egg white

2 tablespoons granulated white
   sugar

Preheat oven to 350°F. Place the pecans in a small mixing bowl. Add enough egg white to coat and moisten the nuts. Add the sugar and combine thoroughly. Spread pecans on a baking sheet and toast in the oven for 10 minutes, or until the coating is dry. Cool to room temperature. Separate the pecans, as they will stick together.

⚛ CARAMELIZED BANANAS ⚛

3 medium bananas
4 tablespoons brown sugar

4 tablespoons unsalted butter
2 tablespoons dark rum

Peel and slice bananas on a bias into ⅓-inch-thick slices. In a medium sauté pan, combine the sugar and butter. Cook over high heat until the mixture is dark brown, thick, and bubbles furiously, about 10 minutes. Add the bananas and cook for 10 seconds. Add the rum to flambé, remove from heat, and spread bananas evenly on a greased baking sheet, reserving the brown sugar caramel. Set aside until needed.

PLEASE NOTE: Flambé only if you are already experienced with this technique. While very impressive, it's not necessary.

⚛ CAJETA ⚛

Cajeta is a traditional Latin caramel made from sugar and goat's milk.

1½ cups granulated white sugar
2 cups milk
2 cups goat's milk

1 teaspoon cornstarch
pinch baking soda

Place ¾ cup of the sugar in a small skillet and melt over medium heat for about 7 minutes, stirring constantly until golden brown and free of lumps. Remove from heat. Combine the two milks and pour about ¼ of mixture (1 cup) into a bowl. Add cornstarch and baking soda, stirring to remove lumps, and set aside. Add the remaining ¾ cup of sugar to the 3 cups remaining milk, and heat in a saucepan over medium heat, stirring occasionally. Bring just to the boiling point and add the caramelized sugar all at once, while stirring vigorously. Add reserved milk-cornstarch mixture and stir well. Reduce heat to low and simmer for 50 to 60 minutes, stirring occasionally. Cajeta will begin to thicken during the last 15 minutes of cooking. Stir more frequently to prevent sticking. Set aside until ready to assemble.

To assemble, place one fried tortilla round in the center of each plate. Place 3 banana slices, with some of the reserved brown sugar caramel, on each tortilla. Spoon 1 tablespoon of the custard over the bananas, followed by several candied pecans. Repeat the procedure for a second layer, topping with the caramelized tortilla round. Spoon the cajeta around the plate. *Serves 4.*

❧ CARIBBEAN CRÈME BRÛLÉE ❧

This crème brûlée is the dessert-equivalent of a piña colada.

1 cup heavy cream
1 cup coconut milk, fresh or
   canned
8 egg yolks
⅓ cup granulated white sugar
1 teaspoon vanilla

¼ cup Malibu rum
¼ cup granulated white sugar
   (for the caramelized tops)
3 tablespoons toasted, sweet-
   ened, flaked coconut
fresh pineapple, if desired

Preheat oven to 300°F. In a large bowl, combine the cream, coconut milk, egg yolks, sugar, vanilla, and rum. Whisk until smooth. Skim off any foam or bubbles. Divide mixture among 6 ramekins or custard cups. Place in a water bath (page 21), and bake until set around the edges, but still loose in the center, about 40 to 50 minutes. Remove from oven and leave in the water bath until cooled. Remove cups from water bath and chill for at least 2 hours, or up to 2 days.

When ready to serve, sprinkle about 2 teaspoons of sugar over each custard. Before caramelizing custards which contain alcohol, please see note in **Tips and Techniques** (page 22). When the top has hardened, sprinkle the toasted coconut evenly over the finished crème brûlée. Serve with fresh pineapple, if desired. *Serves 6.*

NOTE: To toast coconut, spread it out in a thin layer on a baking sheet. Place in a 300°F oven for 10 to 12 minutes, until lightly browned. Shake the baking sheet a few times while toasting, checking often to be sure it doesn't burn.

⚅ GOAT CHEESE CRÈME BRÛLÉE ⚅ WITH PAPAYA SAUCE

Young, talented, and creative Enrico Glaudo, chef-owner of EMI, at 6602 Melrose Avenue in Los Angeles, has invented a most unusual crème brûlée. Not only is it absolutely delicious, but it also makes a lovely and dramatic presentation.

butter, for greasing ramekins
12 egg yolks
½ cup granulated sugar
½ cup (approximately 5 ounces) goat cheese
2 cups heavy cream

¾ cup milk
zest of ½ orange and ½ lemon
1 teaspoon vanilla
¼ cup granulated white sugar (for the caramelized tops)
Papaya Sauce (page 68)

Lightly butter 6 individual ramekins or muffin cups. Beat egg yolks and sugar until light and fluffy. Add the goat cheese and continue to beat until well incorporated. Set aside. In a large, heavy-bottomed saucepan, combine cream, milk, the orange and lemon zest, and vanilla. Bring to a gentle boil. Remove saucepan from heat and strain mixture into a large mixing bowl. Add egg mixture and beat vigorously. Let the mixture rest for about 30 minutes.

Preheat oven to 200°F. With a ladle, skim foam from the top. Divide into ramekins, and place in a paper-towel-lined water bath (page 21). Bake for 2 hours, or until set. Remove from oven and allow to cool. Remove from water bath and refrigerate for at least 2 hours, or up to 2 days.

When ready to serve, unmold the custards, sprinkle the tops with a little sugar, and caramelize using a butane torch for best results. Garnish with the sauce and (optional) fresh berries. Serve immediately, or chill until ready to serve.

❧ PAPAYA SAUCE ❧

1 ripe papaya
sugar, to taste

water
fresh berries of any kind
(optional)

Peel and remove seeds from papaya. Add sugar to taste, though it may not be needed if the papaya is very sweet and ripe. Blend and add water until fruit sauce reaches the desired consistency. Keep chilled until ready to garnish your crème brûlées.

To make the flower design shown, set aside about 2 tablespoons sauce, adding a drop of red food-coloring to darken. Fill a plastic squeeze-style container with the papaya sauce. Squeeze out 6 small pools of sauce around the unmolded custard, then drop a small amount of the reserved red-colored sauce into the center of each. Using a toothpick, drag a line through the center of the flower petal, out toward the rim of the plate. *Serves 6*

❧ Persimmon and Spice Crème Brûlée ❧

Take advantage of persimmons when they're in season. To ripen, place them in the freezer overnight, then thaw; they will be ready to use. Unripe persimmons have an acid taste and will pucker the mouth.

6 eggs
¾ cup granulated white sugar
2 cups half-and-half
1 teaspoon fresh lemon juice
½ teaspoon ground ginger
½ teaspoon ground
  cinnamon

½ teaspoon ground
  allspice
pinch ground cloves
2 to 3 large, ripe persimmons,
  puréed and strained
¼ cup granulated white sugar
  (for the caramelized tops)

Preheat oven to 300°F. Put eggs and sugar in bowl of an electric mixer. Using paddle attachment, beat on medium speed until well combined. Reduce speed to low, and add the half-and-half, lemon juice, ginger, cinnamon, allspice, cloves, and persimmon purée. Mix well. Strain into a large bowl, skimming off any foam or bubbles.

Divide mixture among 6 ramekins or custard cups. Place in a water bath (page 21), and bake until set around the edges, but still loose in the center, about 30 to 40 minutes. Remove from oven and leave in the water bath until cooled. Remove cups from water bath and chill for at least 2 hours, or up to 2 days.

When ready to serve, sprinkle about 2 teaspoons of sugar over each custard. For best results, use a small, hand-held torch to melt sugar. If you don't have a torch, place under the broiler until sugar melts. Rechill custards for a few minutes before serving. *Serves 6.*

∾ PUMPKIN AND SPICE CRÈME BRÛLÉE ∾

As a change of pace for Thanksgiving Day dessert, instead of pumpkin pie, you might consider Pumpkin Crème Brûlée!

2 cups heavy cream
2 teaspoons rum or vanilla
8 egg yolks
⅓ cup granulated white sugar
1 cup puréed pumpkin

¼ teaspoon cinnamon
⅛ teaspoon ground nutmeg
¼ teaspoon ground ginger
¼ cup granulated white sugar
  (for the caramelized tops)

Preheat oven to 300°F. In a large bowl, whisk together the cream, rum or vanilla, yolks, sugar, pumpkin, cinnamon, nutmeg, and ginger. Blend well. Strain into a large bowl, skimming off any foam or bubbles. Divide mixture among 6 ramekins or custard cups. Place in a water bath (page 21), and bake until set around the edges, but still loose in the center, about 30 to 40 minutes. Remove from oven and leave in the water bath until cooled. Remove cups from water bath and chill for at least 2 hours, or up to 2 days.

When ready to serve, sprinkle about 2 teaspoons of sugar over each custard. Before caramelizing custards which contain alcohol, please see note in **Tips and Techniques** (page 22). After caramelizing, re-chill custards for a few minutes before serving.

For an alternative presentation, this crème brûlée could be served in hollowed-out mini pumpkins. *Serves 6.*

❧ SWEET CORN CRÈME BRÛLÉE ❧

Rich and savory, this dish stands alone as a main course served with salad.

2 tablespoons sweet butter
3 large corn cobs or 1½ cups frozen white corn, thawed
6 egg yolks
3 tablespoons granulated white sugar
2 cups light cream, or half-and-half

⅛ teaspoon saffron
2 cups shredded Jack cheese
1 tablespoon crushed dill
½ teaspoon salt
½ teaspoon white pepper
¼ cup granulated white sugar (for the optional caramelized tops)

In a medium saucepan over low heat, melt the butter. If using fresh corn, remove the kernels from the cob. Add the fresh or thawed corn kernels to the saucepan and heat for 2 minutes. Remove from heat and set aside. In a large bowl, whisk the yolks, sugar, cream, saffron, cheese, dill, salt, and pepper until well blended. Transfer the corn to a blender or food processor, and purée until corn is smooth. Add yolk-and-cream mixture to the corn, blending until all ingredients are well combined.

Divide mixture among 6 ramekins or custard cups, or pour into a 2-quart ovenproof casserole dish. Place in a water bath (page 21), and bake until set around the edges, but still loose in the center, about 40 to 50 minutes. Allow more time to set if using the 2-quart casserole dish.

Remove from oven and serve warm. If you choose to caramelize the tops, sprinkle about 2 teaspoons of sugar over each custard. For best results, use a small, hand-held torch to melt sugar. If you don't have a torch, place under the broiler until sugar melts. Allow the custards to cool for a few minutes before serving. *Serves 6.*

❧ GINGER CHILE CRÈME BRÛLÉE ❧

This recipe was developed by Larry Hunter, a scientist at the National Institutes of Health and an accomplished cook, for a potluck gathering of "chileheads" in Washington, D.C. While the name might suggest that this is a savory recipe, it is actually sweet and very spicy.

8 egg yolks
½ cup granulated white sugar
2 cups heavy cream
2 tablespoons orange liqueur, such as Triple Sec or Grand Marnier
2 tablespoons finely-grated gingerroot
2 diced serrano chile peppers
1 dried habañero or ancho chile, seeded and powdered
¼ cup granulated white sugar (for the caramelized tops)

In a large bowl, whisk together egg yolks and sugar until the sugar has dissolved and the mixture is thick and pale yellow. Add the cream, orange liqueur, gingerroot, serrano, and habañero or ancho chiles. Transfer mixture to the top of a double boiler, or a heatproof bowl set over gently simmering water (page 19). Stir constantly for 30 to 45 minutes, or until mixture has thickened enough to coat the back of a wooden spoon. Remove custard from heat and strain into a large, clean bowl. The custard will thicken as it cools. Chill for at least 2 hours, or overnight. Divide custard among 6 ramekins or custard cups.

When ready to serve, sprinkle about 2 teaspoons of sugar over each custard. Before caramelizing custards which contain alcohol, please see note in **Tips and Techniques** (page 22). Re-chill custards for a few minutes before serving. *Serves 6.*

CARAMELIZED MAUI ONION CRÈME BRÛLÉE

Any sweet onion, including Walla Walla and Vidalia, would be delicious in this recipe. This crème brûlée can also be served warm from the oven as a savory side dish that would complement meat or poultry.

1 large Maui onion
3 tablespoons balsamic vinegar
3 tablespoons granulated white sugar
3 tablespoons cooking oil

2 cups heavy cream
6 egg yolks
¼ cup granulated sugar (for the caramelized tops)

Preheat oven to 350°F. Trim off end of onion to level. Place in a small, buttered baking dish. Whisk the balsamic vinegar, sugar, and oil until very well blended. Pour this marinade over the onion. Cover with foil and bake until the onion is very tender, about 1 hour.

Remove from oven and let cool slightly. Transfer onion and 1 tablespoon of the marinade to a blender or food processor. Discard the remaining marinade. Add the cream and purée, being careful not to whip the cream. Add the egg yolks and mix just until blended. Strain into a large bowl, skimming off any foam or bubbles.

Divide mixture among 6 ramekins or custard cups. Place in a water bath (page 21), and bake until set around the edges, but still loose in the center, about 40 to 50 minutes. Remove from oven and leave in the water bath until cooled. Remove cups from water bath and chill for at least 2 hours, or up to 2 days.

When ready to serve, sprinkle about 2 teaspoons of sugar over each custard. For best results, use a small, hand-held torch to melt sugar. If you don't have a torch, place under the broiler until sugar melts. Re-chill custards for a few minutes before serving. *Serves 6*

❧ ROASTED SWEET GARLIC ❧ CRÈME BRÛLÉE

Unusual? Maybe. Delicious? Definitely. Rather than served as a dessert, this recipe makes a savory side dish to roasted meats or poultry.

2 tablespoons unsalted butter
6 cloves of garlic, unpeeled
2 cups heavy cream
4 egg yolks

2 eggs
¼ cup granulated white sugar
   (for the caramelized tops)

Preheat oven to 350°F. In a small, ovenproof pan, melt the butter and add the garlic. Sauté over medium-low heat until the garlic is soft, about 15 minutes. Transfer mixture to oven and bake for 30 minutes. Remove pan from oven, and reduce temperature to 300°F. Squeeze the garlic from its skin and discard skin. Place garlic and cream in a blender and purée, being careful not to whip the cream. Pour the purée into a large bowl. Whisk the egg yolks and whole eggs together, then slowly whisk into the cream mixture; blend well. Season with salt and pepper. Strain into a large bowl, skimming off any foam or bubbles.

Divide mixture among 6 ramekins or custard cups. Place in a water bath (page 21), and bake until set around the edges, but still loose in the center, about 40 to 50 minutes. Remove from oven and leave in water bath until cooled. Remove cups from water bath and chill for at least 2 hours, or up to 2 days.

When ready to serve, sprinkle about 2 teaspoons of sugar over each custard. For best results, use a small, hand-held torch to melt sugar. If you don't have a torch, place under the broiler until sugar melts. Re-chill custards for a few minutes before serving. *Serves 6*

❧ ROASTED RED BELL PEPPER ❧ CRÈME BRÛLÉE

Despite the name, this is actually a sweet crème brûlée. For the photo, I used hollowed-out bell peppers as an alternative to ramekins.

3 red bell peppers
2 cups heavy cream
6 egg yolks
3 tablespoons granulated white sugar
½ teaspoon salt

¼ cup granulated white sugar (for the carmelized tops)
6 small red bell peppers, hollowed out (if using alternative presentation idea)

Preheat broiler. Halve the peppers lengthwise and remove seeds. Place peppers, skin-side up, on a broiler pan. Broil about 3 inches from heat. As the skins blacken, turn peppers until skins are black all over.

Change oven setting to Bake, and reduce temperature to 300°F. Using tongs, transfer the peppers to a plastic zip-close bag. Seal bag and let peppers steam for 15 to 20 minutes. Remove from bag and peel off skins. Place peppers and cream in a blender and purée, being careful not to whip the cream. Strain into a large bowl. Whisk egg yolks, sugar, and salt, then slowly whisk into the cream mixture. Blend well.

Divide mixture among 6 ramekins or custard cups. Place in a water bath (page 21), and bake until set around the edges, but still loose in the center, about 40 to 50 minutes. Remove from oven and leave in the water bath until cooled. Remove cups from water bath and chill for at least 2 hours, or up to 2 days.

When ready to serve, sprinkle about 2 teaspoons of sugar over each custard. For best results, use a small, hand-held torch to melt sugar. If you don't have a torch, place under the broiler until sugar melts. Re-chill custards for a few minutes before serving.

For the alternative presentation, bake custard in one large, oven-proof baking dish and place in water bath. When custard is well-chilled, spoon into the hollowed-out peppers, and caramelize using the torch method only. *Serves 6.*

❧ FLAN ❧

Although flan is a custard-based dessert comparable to crème brûlée, it is usually made with milk and whole eggs, and the caramelizing is the first step instead of the last. This version of flan can be made lighter, if you desire, by using 4 cups of milk instead of the 3 cups of milk and 1 cup of cream.

1¾ cups granulated white sugar
3 cups milk
1 cup heavy cream
5 large whole eggs

5 large egg yolks
1 teaspoon vanilla
mint sprigs for garnish (optional)
fresh fruits for garnish (optional)

In a small, heavy saucepan, dissolve ¾ cup of the sugar in ¼ cup water. Over moderate heat, stir and bring the syrup to a boil. Leave uncovered and undisturbed until it begins to turn golden. Continue to boil, swirling the pan, until syrup is a deep amber or caramel color. Pour immediatcly into a non stick loaf pan, 9x5x3 inches, and swirl pan to coat the bottom and ½ inch up the sides. Let caramel harden.

Preheat oven to 325°F. In another saucepan, scald (heating to just below boiling point, until a skin forms over top) the milk and cream. In a large bowl, whisk together the whole eggs, yolks, and remaining 1 cup sugar. Add scalded milk mixture in a stream while whisking. Stir in vanilla. Pour custard through a fine strainer into the prepared loaf pan.

Set loaf pan into a larger shallow pan or baking dish, and pour hot tap water into the outer pan, until the level reaches halfway up the sides of loaf pan. Cover with a layer of foil and place pan on middle rack of preheated oven. Bake for 1 hour and 10 minutes, or until a knife inserted

1 inch in from the edge comes out clean. Flan will continue to set as it cools. Remove loaf pan from water, and remove foil. Let flan cool on a rack. Cover and chill for at least 3 hours, or up to 1 day, in advance of serving.

Run a thin knife around all sides of the pan, invert a platter over pan, and invert flan onto platter. Arrange fruit around flan and garnish with mint sprigs. Flan is delicious with fresh fruit, such as strawberries, blueberries, sliced peaches, or a combination of fruits. *Serves 8.*

❧ EGGLESS CRÈME CARAMEL ❧

This recipe is a rich and silky version of flan. When unmolded, the caramel drizzles down the sides of the freestanding custard, forming a pool of syrup.

¾ cup granulated white sugar
1 cup milk
3 cups heavy cream
1½ cups powdered sugar

2 tablespoons unflavored gelatin
3 tablespoons brandy
mint sprigs for garnish
fresh fruit, for garnish

In a small, heavy saucepan, dissolve the sugar in ¼ cup water. Over moderate heat, stir and bring the syrup to a boil. Leave uncovered and undisturbed until it begins to turn golden, about 15 minutes. Continue to boil, swirling the pan, until it is a deep amber or caramel color. Pour the caramel immediately into a pan or casserole dish with high sides, approximately 1½- to 2-quart capacity. Let the caramel harden.

In a medium saucepan, combine half of the milk (½ cup), the cream, and powdered sugar. Bring to a boil over medium-low heat.

Meanwhile, in a small bowl, stir gelatin into remaining ½ cup of milk and set aside for 3 minutes, until gelatin is completely dissolved. Remove boiled-milk mixture from heat, and gently stir in gelatin-and-milk mixture, then add brandy. Pour mixture into pan or casserole dish and refrigerate for at least 2 hours, or until mixture is very firm.

Just before serving, run a thin knife around the sides of the pan, invert a platter over pan, and invert custard onto it. Place a slice on each plate, and spoon any remaining caramel sauce over the slices. Garnish with mint sprigs and fresh fruits, such as strawberries, blueberries, blackberries, and peach slices. *Serves 8.*

✎ CROISSANT PUDDING ✎ WITH WHISKEY SAUCE

Bread pudding, which started out as peasant food making the most of leftover bread, becomes elegant simply by upgrading to croissants and serving with Whiskey Sauce, or Apple Brandy Custard Sauce (page 85). You can also substitute egg bread for the croissants.

6 large croissants, sliced in half
  lengthwise
8 large eggs
1 cup granulated white sugar

3 cups cream
2 teaspoons pure vanilla extract
Whiskey Sauce (page 84)

Preheat oven to 350°F. Butter a 9x13-inch baking pan. Layer the croissants in pan, making sure entire surface is covered, with no space between the slices. Whisk eggs and sugar together, and blend well. Whisk in the cream and vanilla. Slowly pour cream mixture over the croissants, allowing the bread to absorb the liquid. You may want to push down the croissants with the back of a spoon so they absorb more of the liquid.

Set baking pan into a larger, shallow pan or baking dish, and pour hot tap water into the outer pan, until the level reaches halfway up the

sides of inner pan. Place on center rack of oven, and bake until pudding is just set, about 45 minutes. Remove from oven, and remove the inner pan from outer pan.

❧ WHISKEY SAUCE ❧

5 large egg yolks
½ cup granulated white sugar

¼ cup Irish whiskey or bourbon

Beat the egg yolks and sugar in large bowl of electric mixer until pale yellow. Add the whiskey and beat until well combined. Transfer mixture to the top of a double boiler, or a heatproof bowl set over simmering water (page 19). Cook, stirring constantly, over medium-high heat until the mixture is thick and creamy. Whisk just before serving.

To serve, place a slice of the pudding (warm or chilled) on a plate, and top with the Whiskey Sauce. *Serves 8.*

❧ APPLE BRANDY CUSTARD SAUCE ❧

This sauce is wonderful either as an option to the Whiskey Sauce over the warm croissant pudding, or spooned over ice cream, poured over pancakes or waffles, or drizzled on baked apples.

4 egg yolks
2 cups milk
¼ cup granulated white sugar

½ teaspoon vanilla extract
2 tablespoons Calvados or other
   apple brandy

In a bowl, whisk the egg yolks until blended. In a saucepan over medium-high heat, combine the milk and sugar, and heat until sugar has dissolved. When the mixture begins to simmer, remove from heat and slowly whisk it into the yolks. Pour mixture back into saucepan, and return to a medium heat. Cook, stirring constantly, until mixture thickens, about 4 minutes. Stir in the vanilla and brandy.

Serve warm, or keep covered and refrigerated until ready to use. *Yields about 3 cups of sauce.*

⮾ Sugarless Maple Custard ⮾

Lisa M. Carruthers, Master of Science in Consumer and Family Sciences and a registered dietitian, developed this recipe especially for this book. Specializing in cardiac and oncology nutrition, Lisa frequently lectures on nutrition, and also consults with chefs and restaurants on menu development.

2 teaspoons maple extract
2 teaspoons vanilla extract
2 whole eggs
2 cups nonfat milk

2 teaspoons liquid sugar
  substitute
3 tablespoons sugarless maple
  syrup

Preheat oven to 350°F. Heat maple and vanilla extracts in a small saucepan until bubbling. Divide equally into four ramekins or custard dishes. Whisk together the eggs, milk, sugar substitute, and maple syrup until well blended. Pour into prepared custard dishes.

Place ramekins in a water bath (page 21) and bake until set, about 40 minutes. Remove from oven and leave in the water bath until cooled. Remove cups from water bath and chill for at least 2 hours, or up to 2 days.

When ready to serve, unmold the custards onto a dessert plate. *Serves 4.*

❧ Rice Pudding ❧

Rice pudding is the quintessential comfort food.

2 cups water
¼ teaspoon salt
1 cup uncooked medium- or
   long-grain rice
2 cups whole milk

3 cups half-and-half
⅔ cup granulated white sugar
1½ teaspoons pure vanilla
   extract

Bring 2 cups water to a boil in large, heavy-bottomed pot. Stir in salt and rice. Cover and simmer over low heat until water is almost fully absorbed, about 15 to 20 minutes.

Add milk, half-and-half, and sugar. Increase heat to medium-high to bring to a simmer, then reduce heat to maintain simmer. Cook uncovered, stirring frequently, until mixture starts to thicken, about 30 minutes. Reduce heat to low and continue to cook, stirring every few minutes to prevent sticking, until mixture is thick and all liquid has been absorbed, about 10 minutes. Remove from heat and stir in vanilla extract.

Spoon into serving dish or individual custard cups. Serve warm, room temperature, or chilled. *Serves 8 to 10.*

≈ RICE PUDDING ≈
ARROZ DULCE STYLE

Arroz dulce means sweet rice in Spanish. This version is very popular in Mexico and, in fact, is the way I was first introduced to it by my mother-in-law.

Follow directions for Rice Pudding, increasing sugar to 1½ cups and adding ½ cup raisins or other dried fruit and 1 teaspoon ground cinnamon, along with vanilla extract.

As a pleasant surprise for your special guests, serve your desserts in pretty edible shells, boxes, or bowls. They can be made far in advance if desired, but must be tightly covered and kept dry and cool. I firmly believe that high-quality chocolate is worth the price difference. It will always give the best results. For specific instructions about melting chocolate, see **Tips and Techniques** (page 23).

Six ounces of melted chocolate will yield enough for 6 servings in each of the next four presentation ideas:

CHOCOLATE CUPS

Pour cooled melted chocolate into paper (cupcake) baking cups. Spread chocolate evenly inside the cups with a brush or spoon. Let stand until set, then add another layer of chocolate. Refrigerate until the second layer is set, then peel away the paper cups.

CHOCOLATE SHELLS

Shell shapes make beautiful containers for custards. Simply cover scallop-shell molds or large seashells with plastic wrap, then brush with an even layer of cooled, melted chocolate. Let stand until hardened, then carefully peel away plastic wrap.

Chocolate Boxes

Line a baking sheet with waxed paper. Pour cooled melted chocolate onto the waxed paper, spreading to a square about 12"x12". Chill until set. (This can be done far in advance and kept chilled.) When set, use a sharp knife to score the chocolate into equal-size squares to form the sides of the boxes, and assemble using additional melted chocolate as your glue. Fill the boxes with custard, pressing very lightly so the edges line up equally (photo, page 48).

Graham Cracker Chocolate Cups

Brush an even layer of cooled, melted chocolate inside single-serve graham cracker crusts.

Easy Chocolate Bowls

This presentation idea uses balloons in a rather unique way. If this is the first time you have made these bowls, expect to get about 6 usable bowls from this recipe. Although you would have enough chocolate to make 10, some of the bowls may break and some may not be very attractive.

2 teaspoons vegetable oil or
   shortening
8 to 10 small, round
   balloons

10 ounces good-quality
   bittersweet chocolate

Inflate balloons to 3 inches at widest point. Cover a baking sheet with waxed paper. Pour the oil onto a plate with a rim. Dip hands in oil and lightly rub over the bottom two-thirds of each balloon, starting at the end opposite the tied end. (You can grease three balloons with each dip of the hands in oil.) Rub balloons gently with a clean dish towel or paper towel to remove excess oil; if there is too much oil on the balloon, the chocolate won't stick. Place balloons on baking sheet.

In the dry top of a double boiler, or in a heatproof bowl set over simmering water (page 19), melt chocolate, stirring frequently. Be sure no water gets into the chocolate or it will seize and become grainy. When chocolate has melted, remove from heat and allow it to cool. Balloons will pop if the chocolate is too hot.

When making the bowls, it is easiest to work with one balloon at a time. Holding the tied end in your fingers, dip each balloon about a third of the way up its sides into melted chocolate. Remove balloon from the chocolate and place it, tied-end up, on baking sheet lined with waxed paper.

To create a flower effect, place the bottom of the balloon in the pot of chocolate and rock the balloon away from you, then toward you. Turn balloon 90 degrees and repeat. Try to make each swing of the balloon even, so that each of the four petal shapes will be symmetrical. Repeat until six balloons have been dipped and placed on a waxed-paper-covered baking sheet.

Chill baking sheet in refrigerator for 15 minutes. Continue with as many of the remaining balloons as you can dip. If there is too little chocolate left for dipping, use a pastry brush to paint the chocolate onto the balloons.

When ready to fill, remove from refrigerator and, with a sharp knife (or pin), pop the balloon and carefully remove. Fill chocolate bowls and serve immediately, or keep in refrigerator for up to three days. *Yields about 6 to 8.*

≋ TULIP SHELLS ≋

These easy-to-make shells are a great way to use up all those egg whites!

1 cup egg whites
1 cup powdered sugar
1 cup melted sweet butter

1 teaspoon pure vanilla extract
¾ cup flour

Combine the egg whites, sugar, butter, and vanilla extract in the bowl of a processor. Sift in flour and process until combined. Pour mixture into a bowl and chill for 2 hours. This batter can be prepared 1 to 2 days in advance.

Preheat oven to 350°F. Assemble 4 small bowls, cups, or ramekins that fit into each other. Pour a heaping tablespoon of batter onto a non-stick baking sheet or jellyroll pan. The mixture will spread into a circle. Repeat and make a second circle. Bake for 10 minutes.

Turn two bowls upside down. Lift hot pastry circles from baking sheet and place one circle over the bottom of each inverted bowl. Cover each circle with a second bowl. Press down gently to form the tulip-shell shape. Let cool. Remove shells from bowls and place on a flat surface. Continue baking in pairs until all batter is used.

Fill the tulip shells with chilled custard. If caramelizing, use the torch method only, wrapping aluminum foil over the edges of tulip shells to prevent burning. Chill until ready to serve. *Yields about 2 dozen.*

❧ MOLASSES TAQUITOS ❧

Delicate and crisp, Molasses Taquitos complement the contrasting smooth, creamy custard very nicely. For the filling, use the Classic Crème Brûlée, Stirred Method (page 27), piping it into the taquitos using a pastry bag fitted with a fluted tip.

½ cup (1 stick) unsalted butter	½ cup flour
½ cup molasses	¼ teaspoon salt
4 tablespoons granulated white sugar	¼ teaspoon cinnamon
	¼ teaspoon ground ginger
2 egg whites, beaten	¼ teaspoon ground cloves

Preheat oven to 350°F. Line two baking sheets with parchment paper or aluminum foil, or use a non-stick baking sheet. In a medium saucepan over medium heat, melt the butter, molasses, and sugar. Remove from heat and allow to cool for about 3 minutes before adding egg whites; if mixture is too hot, they will scramble. Add egg whites, blending well. Reduce heat to very low, to prevent mixture from becoming too thick. Sift the flour, salt, cinnamon, ginger, and cloves over the molasses mixture, blending well.

Drop heaping tablespoons of the mixture, 4 inches apart, on baking sheet. With the back of a spoon, spread into a circle, about 3 or 4 inches in diameter. Bake for about 7 minutes, or until bubbly. Remove from oven and allow to cool 1 minute. Carefully lift the hot cookie with a spatula, and drape it over the handle of a large wooden spoon. Roll the cookie around the handle, overlapping the edges to make a cylinder, and press down on the seam for a few seconds to seal the shape (photo, page

89). Cool on a wire rack. Repeat with the remaining mixture. Store taquitos in an airtight container, away from heat, until ready to pipe in the custard. *Yields 2 dozen.*

≈ Botanical Ice Bowls ≈

These bowls only seem complicated—they are actually very easy to make and fun to design. They can even be made weeks in advance and kept frozen. If using flowers, consider nasturtiums, lavender, chamomile, geraniums, honeysuckle, pansies, violets, rose petals, or any other non-poisonous flower. If you prefer to use herbs, dill, thyme, marjoram, or rosemary are all suitable.

assorted flowers and/or herbs   water
2 glass bowls with a size   masking tape
   difference of 1 to 2 inches

Start by placing a few flowers or herbs on the bottom of the larger bowl. Place the smaller bowl inside the larger bowl, center, and slowly fill the space between the two with water. Add more herbs and/or flowers in any pattern you like, using a wooden skewer, a spatula, or any thin implement, to push them down into the space, or crevice.

Secure the smaller bowl in the center of the larger bowl, using a strip of masking tape across the lip edges of both bowls to ensure that the smaller stays centered. Place bowls in freezer until frozen, about 4 hours.

Some pieces will likely rise to the surface of the ice bowl as it freezes. If you prefer that they remain below the lip, you may want to first fill the crevice to about ¾ of its available capacity. When that freezes, add more water, filling to just below the lip of the smaller bowl, and refreeze.

Remove bowls from freezer, and let stand for about 5 minutes. When the ice has loosened from the glass, remove tape and lift out the smaller bowl. Remove ice bowl from larger glass bowl, and return it to freezer until ready to use.

These bowls can be used to serve any of the custards, and will definitely ensure an ice-cold dessert. To avoid the custard seeping through, line the bottom of the ice bowl with an edible barrier, such as a wafer, a slice of cake, fruit, or even a thin layer of chocolate. Caramelize using the variation method described on page 22. (Photo, page 52.)